The Littlest Raindrop

Written by Nancy Reiter-Parrish
Illustrated by Kayla Bol

Published by White Feather Press. (www.whitefeatherpress.com)

ISBN 978-1-61808-139-1

Printed in the United States of America

White Feather Press

Reaffirming Faith in God, Family and Country

Dedication

<u>Nancy Parrish</u>

Dedicated to "My littlest sister."
Missie Benner

<u>Kayla Bol</u>

For Emily and Olivia. I am so thankful God blessed me with you as my little sisters!

Rhinehart was a raindrop.

He lived far, far up in the sky
on a cloud with his mother
and father and
many other raindrops.

But Rhinehart was the littlest
of them all.

Rhinehart's father was the leader
of all the other raindrops on
his cloud.

When the time came for the rain
to fall on the earth below, it was
his job to select which
raindrops could go and
which ones had to
stay behind.

Rhinehart was never chosen
to go. His father said he was
too little. And so all Rhinehart
could do was sadly look on as
the other raindrops fell
to the earth.

Oh, how he wished he was
one of them! What fun it
would be to fall through the air
and see the earth up close.

One day after he had watched his father send off the latest group of raindrops, Rhinehart thought to himself,

"I don't care if my father won't send me. I'll go myself! I've got to see the world before I'm too old!"

And before you could say "cats and dogs," Rhinehart was running toward the edge of the cloud!

But Rhinehart's father
had seen him!

"Rhinehart!"

he called in a deep, booming
voice, just as Rhinehart was
about to jump.

"What do you think you're doing?"
"Why, I was just going to... ah, um,"
Rhinehart stammered looking down.
"You know I've told you a hundred
times, you're too little to go
down there, son. You wouldn't
know what to do. Now I don't
ever want to see you try that
foolishness again.

"Remember,"
he added a little more kindly
as he turned to walk away, "you
<u>are</u> the littlest raindrop."

Oh, how Rhinehart hated that word. "Littlest." When was he going to be the big- gest? And as he walked away, pout- ing, he promised himself that the very next chance he had, he would show his father that he could do anything any other raindrop could do and maybe do it even better!

And so the very next day, while
Rhinehart's father was seeing off
another crew of raindrops,
Rhinehart tip-toed very
quietly and quickly
(if raindrops can tip-toe)
to the farthest corner of the cloud
(if clouds have corners)
and jumped off!
"Whee, this is fun!" he cried.

But wait, he was going much
too fast! "Oh dear, Help!" he cried.
And where was he going to land?
He hadn't thought of that.
"Oh dear.

HELP! HELP!"

And then he landed.
"Kerplop!"
Right in the middle of a big
puddle on the sidewalk!

"HELP! HELP!"

He cried,
I can't swim! I'm drowning!"

Then someone had a hold
of him by the shoulders
(if raindrops have shoulders)
and was pulling him upright.

It was Amos, one of the elder
drops. Was Rhinehart ever glad
to see him! And he began to
tell Amos about his adventure
of falling through the air.

But Amos just said, "Rhinehart. You just
wouldn't listen to your father, would you?
Don't you realize
what a good thing it is you
landed where someone
could help you?"

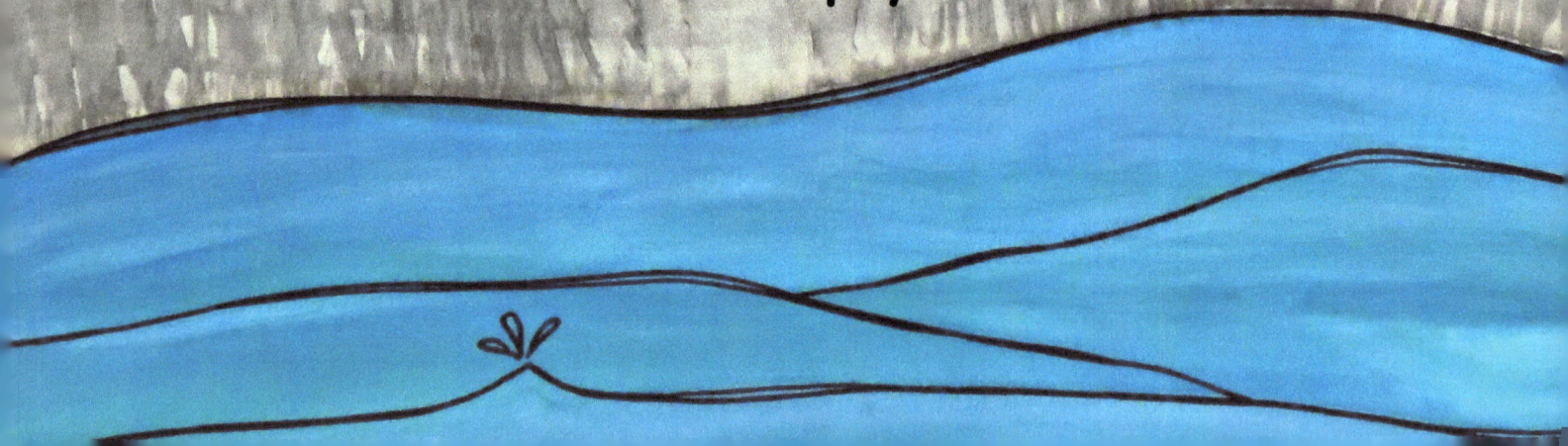

Rhinehart was silent.

"Well, now that you're here, you'll just have to stay," Amos sighed.

"You mean forever?" Rhinehart cried.

"No," chuckled Amos. "Just until morning when the sun comes up and brings us back to our cloud."

Well, Rhinehart had never spent a more miserable night in his entire life! It was cold! And there were so many strange noises! And even though Amos let him sleep on his big, strong back, he was still afraid. And he still missed his mother and father and his bed back home. Rhinehart thought morning would never come.

But it did. The sun rose and smiled on the puddle on the sidewalk. And slowly, one by one, the raindrops began to rise up, up, up until soon the puddle was completely gone! Rhinehart held tight to Amos as they traveled higher and higher.

At last they were home!
My, but is was good to be on
familiar ground again. My,
but it was good to see
his parents again!

And you can be <u>quite</u> sure that the littlest raindrop was <u>quite</u> content to stay <u>quite</u> close to home for <u>quite</u> a while after that!

THE END

THE WATER CYCLE

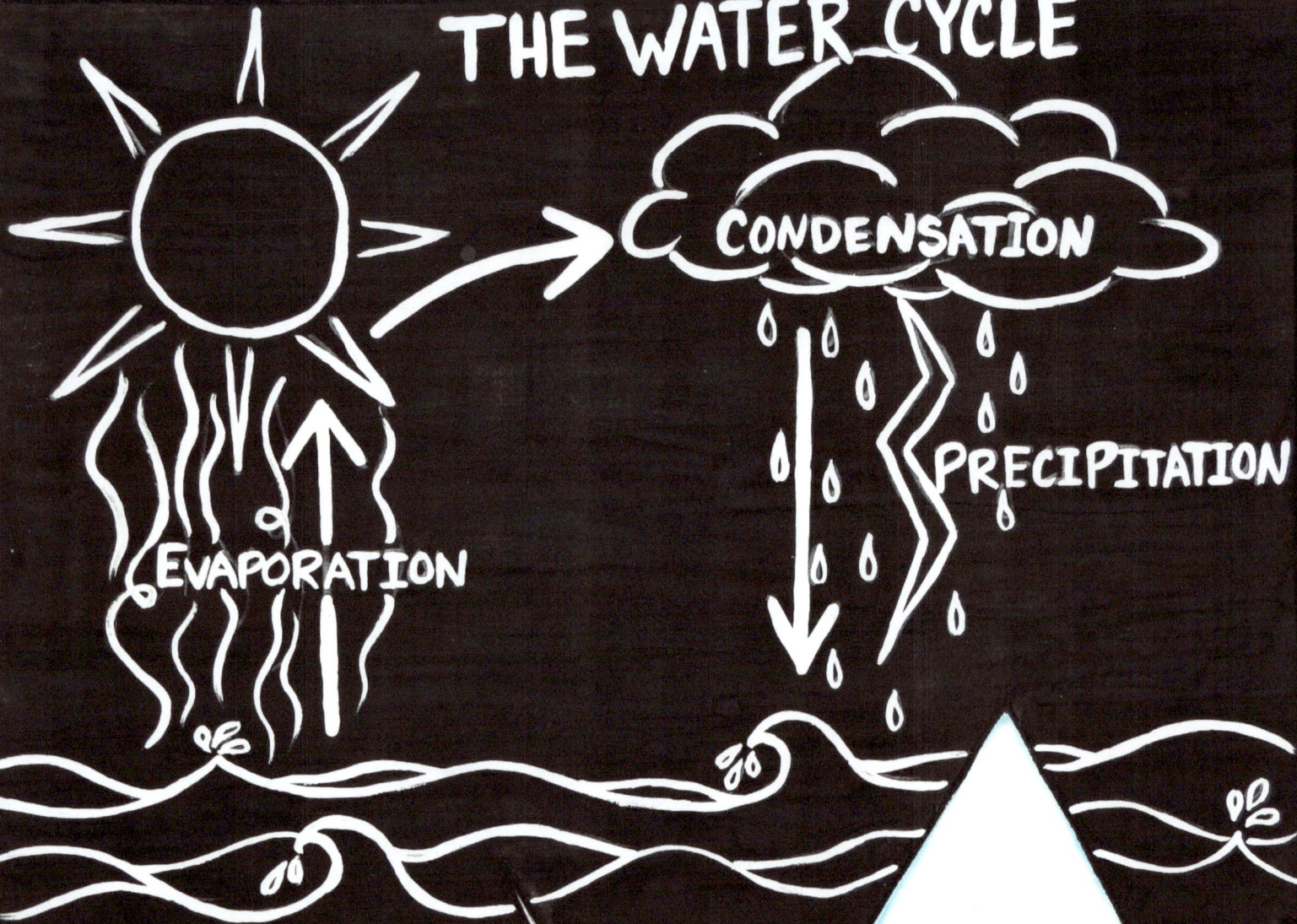

CONDENSATION

PRECIPITATION

EVAPORATION

Hi kids! My name is Professor Whet. Today we're going to be learning about water. Now water may seem pretty simple, but there's more to it than you might imagine. Did you know that water can actually exist in 3 different forms?

When water is warm it is a liquid. This is how most of us picture water. Now if that water starts to get really hot, it turns into steam, which is a gas. This is called evaporation [ih-vap-uh-rey-shuh n]. This is what causes the raindrops in our story to leave the earth and return to the clouds. The sun warms them up, and those raindrops evaporate into steam which rises into the air. Up to 90% of the water in the air comes from water that has evaporated from rivers, lakes, or the ocean.

When the steam gets really high, it begins to cool down. When steam cools down enough it turns back into a liquid. This process is called condensation [kon-den-sey-shuh n]. When steam condenses in the sky, it turns into tiny water droplets that are so small and light they can actually float in the air. When enough of these tiny droplets group together they turn into clouds. So when you look up into the sky and see a cloud, you're actually seeing thousands of us tiny water droplets living together. Then, when it's time to rain, those droplets combine into bigger drops of water that are too heavy to float in the air anymore, so they fall to the earth as rain.

When water gets really cold it actually turns into a solid. It freezes and becomes ice or snow. Later, when the ice or snow warms back up, it turns into liquid water again. Water is constantly changing form between these 3 states: liquid, solid, gas. Remember, water never really disappears, it simply changes form.

KIDS!

What have we learned?

Please complete the following questions by circling "true" or "false." Then your parents will check your answers.

1. Water can take 3 forms.
    True
    False
2. The littliest raindrop is named "Braveheart."
    True
    False
3. When water gets hot, it turns into steam.
    True
    False
4. When the littliest raindrop jumped off the cloud, he was disobeying his parents.
    True
    False
5. Condensation happens when steam cools down and turns back into water.
    True
    False

Certificate of Completion

This certificate is awarded to

_____

and shows they know all about raindrops, about being little and about how to obey Mom and Dad!

Certified Smart!

Additional copies of this book may be purchased at www.amazon.com

www.ingramcontent.com/pod-product-compliance
Lightning Source LLC
LaVergne TN
LVHW072110070426
835509LV00002B/102